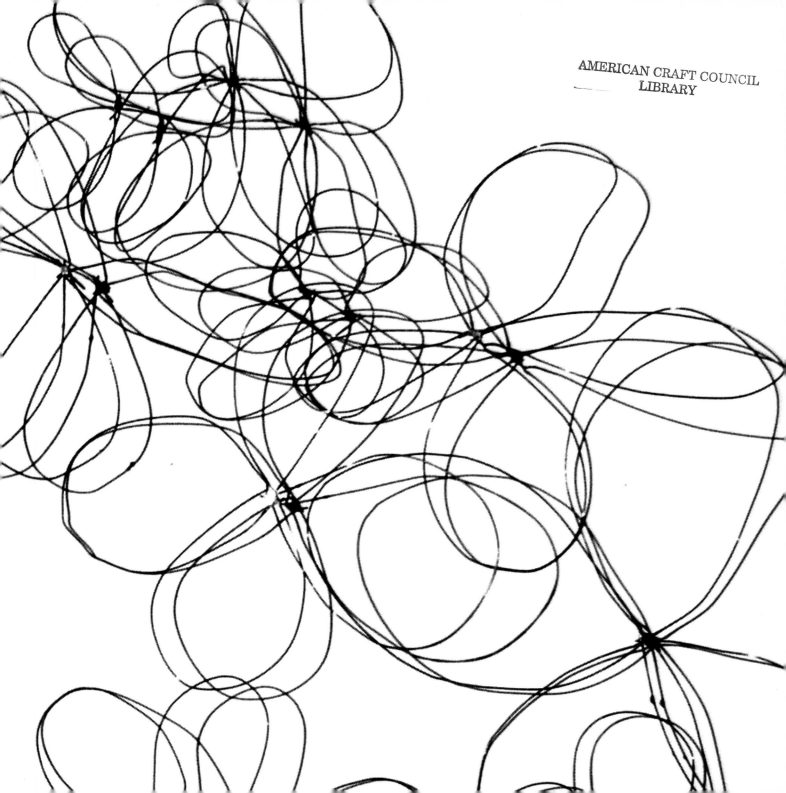

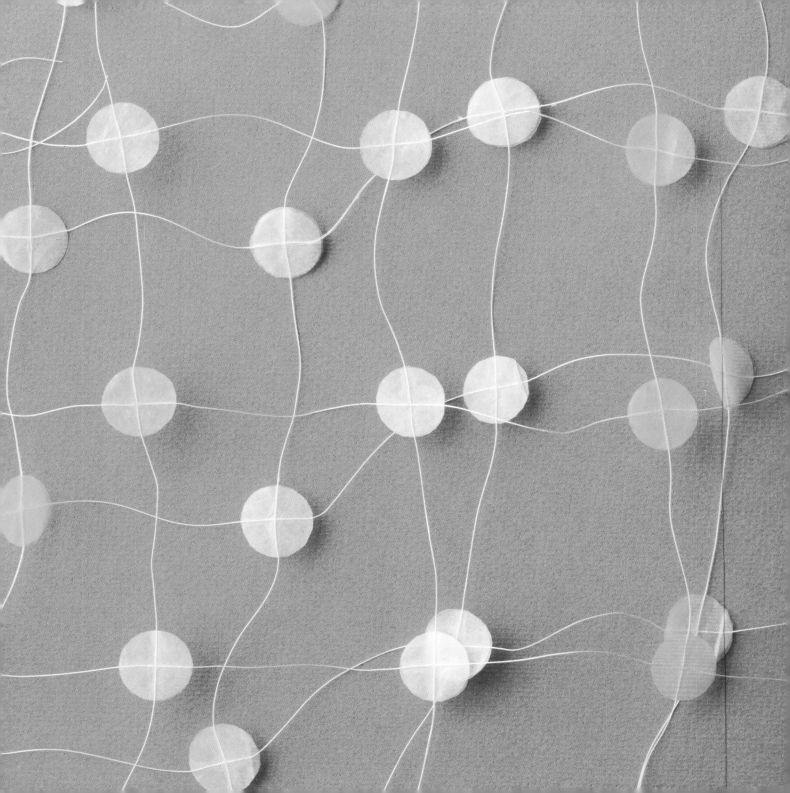

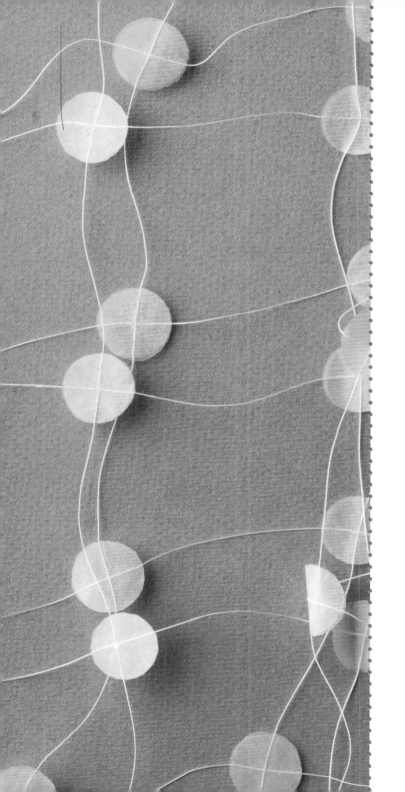

HANGING
IN BALANCE
42 contemporary necklaces

Organized by the Stanlee and Gerald Rubin
Center for the Visual Arts
at the University of Texas at El Paso

This publication accompanies the exhibition *Hanging in Balance: Forty-two Contemporary Necklaces* which was organized by the Stanlee and Gerald Rubin Center for the Visual Arts at the University of Texas at El Paso and curated by Kate Bonansinga and Rachelle Thiewes.

Published by

Stanlee and Gerald Rubin Center for the Visual Arts
The University of Texas at El Paso
El Paso, TX 79968
www.utep.edu/arts

Exhibition itinerary

Stanlee and Gerald Rubin Center for the Visual Arts
The University of Texas at El Paso
and Adair Margo Gallery
El Paso, TX
January 20-March 10, 2005

Southwest School of Art and Craft
San Antonio, TX
June 16-August 14, 2005

Mobilia Gallery
Cambridge, MA
November 1-December 15, 2005

The exhibition and its associated programming in El Paso have been generously supported by the Texas Commission on the Arts, the University of Texas at El Paso and Anne and Sam Davis.

The catalogue was funded in its entirety by the Rotasa Foundation.

ISBN number 0-9760154-2-0
Library of Congress Control Number: 2004115991

Photography credits by page

I, 42, 43, 64	Bettina Dittlmann and Michael Jank
II-III, 24, 41	Marty Snortum
V, 15, 56	Doug Yaple
VI, 26-27, 34	Luke Patrick
8, 22, 48	Frank Hills
9, 58, 59	Tom McInvalle
10-11, 38	Julian Kirschler
12-13, 30-31, 47	Mark Johann
14, 36-37	Norman Watkins
19, 61	Helga Schulze-Brinkop
21, 44	Michael O'Neill
28, 52	Shannon Tofts
32, 51	Maria Hanson
16, 55 (left)	Jörg Fahlenkamp
55 (right)	Silke Mayer

Image credits

All dimensions listed in inches. Dimensions may vary depending on if and how piece is worn.
Inside front and back covers, I, 64: Bettina Dittlmann, *Four Leaf Clover,* detail. Iron, silver solder, 2004, 17 H X 14 W.
II-III: Cynthia Cousens, *White on White (Necklace Study),* detail. Paper, linen, 2004, 63 H X 13½ W X ¼ D.
V: Maria Phillips, *Flush,* detail. Steel, 18kt gold, gut, thread, 2004, 20 H X 10 W X 2 D.
VI: Maru Almeida, *Formation III: Entangle.* Hand-felted wool, peridot, 2004, 12 H X 7 W X 1 D.

Printed by Guynes Printing Company of Texas, Inc.
Designed by Anne M. Giangiulio

HANGING

IN BALANCE:
42 contemporary necklaces

Table of Contents

Foreword

Hanging in Balance: Forty-Two Contemporary Neck-laces is an exhibit of avant-garde jewelry created by fourteen artists from England, Germany, Mexico and the United States. Two necklaces by each artist will be on view at UTEP's splendid new exhibition facility, the Stanlee and Gerald Rubin Center for the Visual Arts. The other necklace by each artist will be displayed at the Adair Margo Gallery in downtown El Paso, one of the major commercial art galleries in West Texas. This partnership with the Adair Margo Gallery will provide an opportunity for client development for the artists, as well as for a more extensive audience for the exhibit. Following its premier in El Paso, the exhibition will travel to other venues in the United States.

All of the pieces are one-of-a-kind art works made by women artists. In the countries represented in this exhibition, jewelry is and always has been worn primarily

Nora Fok, *Hanging in Balance*, Nylon, acrylic balls, 2004, 20 Diameter.

by women, giving the makers and wearers of these necklaces common ground based on gender. These necklaces have the ability to affect the wearer's body posture and, consequently, her relationship with her internal and external worlds.

I express my thanks to the artists for their innovative creations; to Rachelle Thiewes, Professor of Art at UTEP and Kate Bonansinga, director of the Rubin Center for the Visual Arts, for selecting the fourteen artists; and to Adair Margo for opening her gallery to this exhibition. This is the second time that Rachelle Thiewes and Kate Bonansinga have collaborated to bring a jewelry exhibition to UTEP, the first being *The Ring*, a traveling jewelry exhibition organized by Mobilia Gallery.

In addition, I wish to thank Ursula Ilse-Neuman, curator at the Museum of Arts and Design in New York City, for her insightful essay in this publication. I also thank those at UTEP — including Gregory Elliott, chairman of the Department of Art, and Howard Daudistel, dean of the College of Liberal Arts — who have consistently supported the university's quest to increase the profile of the visual arts. Finally, I want to thank the Texas Commission on the Arts for its ongoing support of artistic and cultural products in El Paso, and the Rotasa Foundation, which generously funded this publication in its entirety.

Diana S. Natalicio
President
The University of Texas at El Paso

Anika Smulovitz, *White Collar #4*. Men's white shirt collars, 2003, 13 H X 12 W X 12 D.

The Necklace

Rachelle Thiewes

Necklaces are traditionally thought of as a decorative chain or a string of jewels worn around the neck. Each of the fourteen artists invited to exhibit in *Hanging in Balance: Forty-Two Contemporary Necklaces* break from this tradition and reconsider the necklace as a jewelry form that has the possibility to tightly wrap the entire neck, drape over the shoulders or hang long on the body. They understand the relationship between the necklace as object and its placement on the human figure. It can emphasize or delineate the body's shape as well as control or flow with its

Iris Bodemer, *No. 04-001*, Bronze, rose quartz, coral, citrine, pyrite, bone, 2004, 4½ H X 10 W X 2½ D.

movements. Committed to the study and making of necklaces, this international group of artists brings a fresh and innovative approach to its form, content and material choice. For this exhibition they have made provocative works of art using a variety of materials including wool, nylon and pearls, gut and thread, as well as the traditional jewelry materials: gold, silver and precious stones. Made with expert craftsmanship this group of forty-two necklaces challenges us to think beyond our preconceptions, as the necklace can be so much more than a simple string of jewels.

Striking Balances
Ursula Ilse-Neuman

Jewelry unites the maker and the wearer in what is probably the most intimate of collaborations in contemporary art. The jewelry artist creates a wearable object that is charged with ideas; the object and the ideas bind the wearer to the maker; and the wearer carries the message to a larger audience to complete the artistic vision. In translating their ideas into physical reality, jewelry makers perform the quintessential artistic balancing act, a feat made all the more challenging when concepts are presented in wearable form.

Materials are the crucial mediators in an object's transformation from the imagined to the actual. The artists whose necklaces are included in *Hanging in Balance* capitalize on the structural as well as the aesthetic qualities of all manner of "stuff" to create their profoundly individualistic statements. Unlike their predecessors in the 1960s and 1970s who rejected precious gems and metals,[1] and in contrast to jewelers for centuries prior to that who favored rare materials above all others, today's artists express themselves through a virtually limitless array of synthetic as well as natural materials, including aluminum, rubber, industrial plastics, glass, paper, straw, and found objects — as well as gold, silver and diamonds. This inclusive range of materials marks a fundamental change in the very definition of jewelry from value closely associated with social and economic status to value derived from the ideas expressed.

For most jewelry artists, wearability is a not a constraint. Although fashioning an object that can be worn necessitates concessions to physical reality and the human form, artists accept these restrictions in much the same spirit that poets accept a rhyming scheme. The most direct influence on the design of a necklace is gravity, a

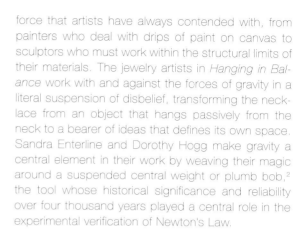

Sandra Enterline, *Untitled*, Silver, seed pearls, 2004, hanging length: 20.

force that artists have always contended with, from painters who deal with drips of paint on canvas to sculptors who must work within the structural limits of their materials. The jewelry artists in *Hanging in Balance* work with and against the forces of gravity in a literal suspension of disbelief, transforming the necklace from an object that hangs passively from the neck to a bearer of ideas that defines its own space. Sandra Enterline and Dorothy Hogg make gravity a central element in their work by weaving their magic around a suspended central weight or plumb bob,[2] the tool whose historical significance and reliability over four thousand years played a central role in the experimental verification of Newton's Law.

At the opposite end of the spectrum, Nora Fok employs synthetic materials to make large, fanciful neckpieces that appear to defy gravity.[3] Her buoyant inventions of lightweight clear and dyed nylon monofilament and acrylic balls seem to float around the neck. Despite her use of traditional metals, Bettina Dittlmann also upsets our expectations by using filigree work as light as spun sugar to form neckpieces that hover in space.

Artists must also consider kinetic forces resulting from the movement of the body in balancing the compositional elements of their necklaces. Such considerations are integral to Maria Hanson's neckpieces in which gravity and movement animate the disparate, free-hanging objects that she draws together using cables and simple forms, and they also define Sandra Enterline's necklaces, which depend on the wearer to add the effects of movement and changing light. In contrast, Jan Baum sidesteps both kinetic forces and gravity and carries the concept of wearability a step further by exploring the boundary between being "in the skin" like a tattoo and being "on top of the skin."

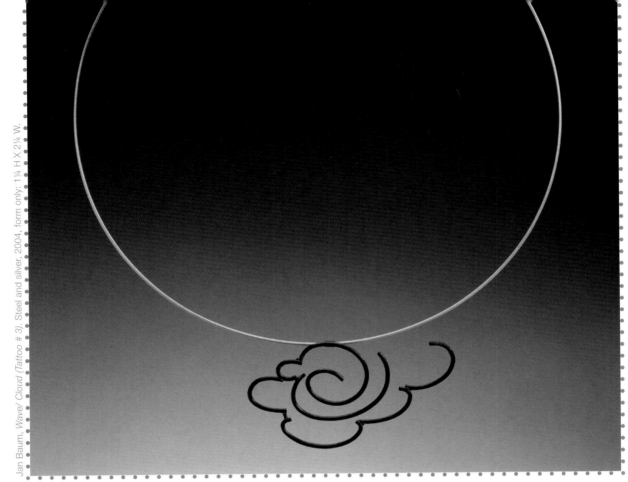

Jan Baum, *Wave/ Cloud (Tattoo # 3)*, Steel and silver, 2004, form only: 1¼ H X 2¼ W.

Bilateral symmetry, another attribute of the material world that affects approaches to jewelry design, is deeply rooted in the human body and mind through evolution. While most of the necklaces in *Hanging in Balance* feature bilateral symmetry, those of Iris Bodemer, Cynthia Cousens, Maria Phillips, Bettina Dittlmann, and Maria Hanson create balances between asymmetric, even amorphous, forms to produce neckpieces that complement the body. In fact, organic and flowing shapes, rather than angular, mechanistic structures such as are commonly associated with masculine imagery, characterize the works in the exhibition. In this light, it is no accident that all of the artists in *Hanging in Balance* are women.

Asymmetry is also behind the sense of unease that underlies Andrea Wippermann's necklaces. Her constructions exude both a timeless, enigmatic quality that alludes to a lost technological society and a sense of mystery and power that makes them emblematic of the will to survive. In this regard, her work joins with the earliest talismanic forms of jewelry.

The metamorphosis and decay of material over time is an aspect of the natural world that is also incorporated into the concepts of some of the neckpieces in *Hanging in Balance*. Maria Phillips examines the processes of inexorable change on both organic and manmade materials in her necklaces. In one example, she wraps

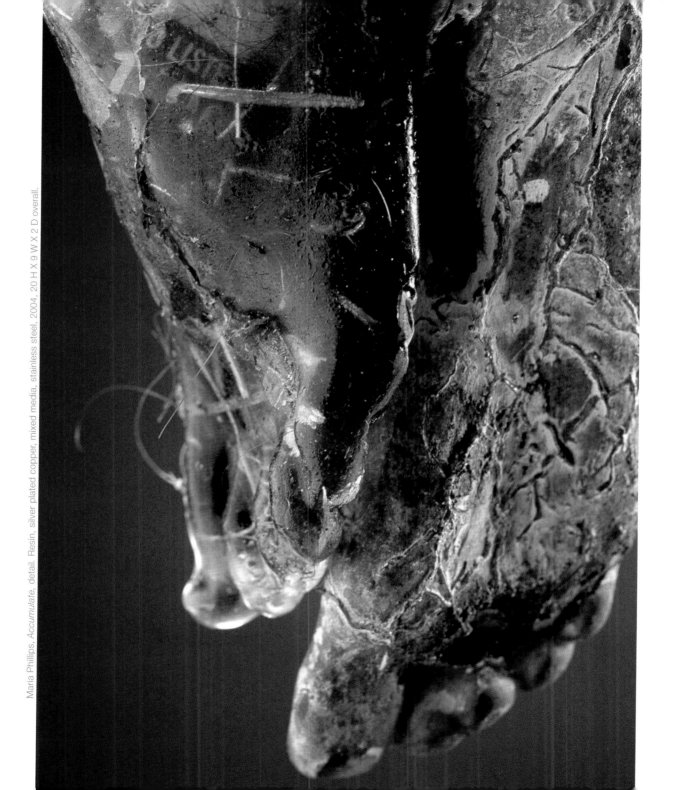

Maria Phillips, *Accumulate*, detail. Resin, silver plated copper, mixed media, stainless steel, 2004, 20 H X 9 W X 2 D overall.

15

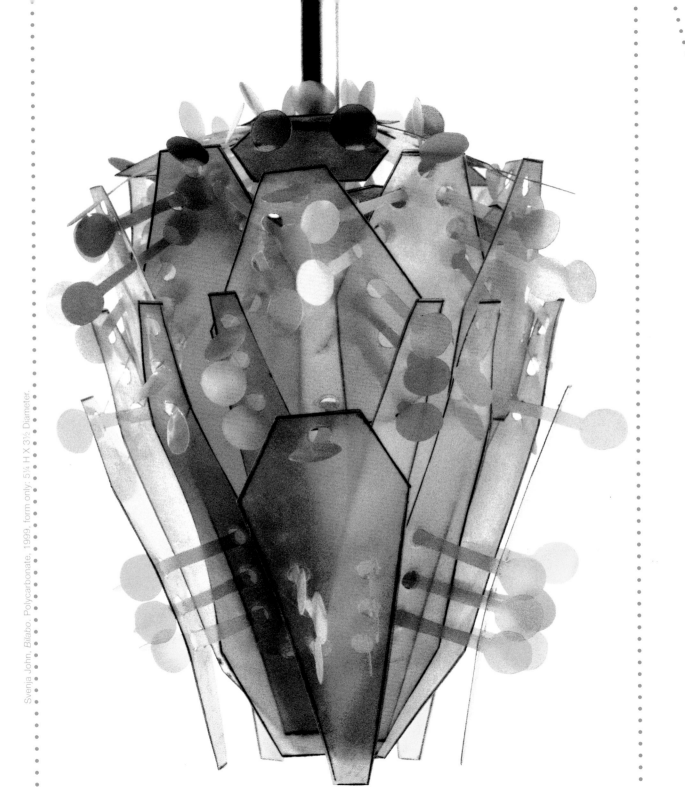

Svenja John, *Bilabo*. Polycarbonate, 1999, form only: 5¼ H X 3½ Diameter.

industrial materials in pig intestine in order to investigate the changes caused by environmental agents. This creates a sense of tension and an ongoing stake in the outcome for both jewelry maker and wearer.

Issues of impermanence and transformation are similarly at the heart of the work of Maru Almeida, who creates jewelry from such disparate materials as precious metals, felt, and sugar, a substance that disintegrates upon wearing. By using sugar, Almeida integrates her jewelry into the processes of life itself, making each piece an intimate representation of inner life and outward appearance. Whether ephemeral (a subversion of the traditional notion of permanence as an integral element of jewelry) or soft and tactile, her jewelry heightens the wearer's experience of the moment when it is worn.

Over the centuries, the manner in which nature is perceived has changed the way artists portray the world around them. In our own age, scientific and technological discoveries are affording us fresh and often startling insights into the architecture and functioning of the universe, from the microscopic to the galactic levels. We now know that the deterministic laws that fueled the Enlightenment and Industrial Revolution break down at the subatomic level and the cause-and-effect rules governing motion and structure are no longer simple or even intuitive.

Through far-reaching mathematical approaches that encourage a more holistic view of nature, we have reached a new understanding over the last several decades of the balance of order and chaos. Whereas traditional mathematical modeling cannot accurately portray the complexities of natural phenomena, new theories provide profound insight into how apparently random forms and events unfold.[4] A major breakthrough is the computer-generated fractal geometry of Benoit Mandelbrot (b. 1924), which has given us a new understanding of the balance of order and chaos in the physical world.

Fractal geometry, by revealing the underlying living, mathematical structure of nature, allows us to comprehend the irregular yet patterned aspects of the physical world. If such natural forms as clouds, mountains, coastlines, tree bark, and lightning are more comprehensible through fractal imagery, then, so, too, are the strange, tortuous, and wrinkled forms fabricated by jewelry artists Iris Bodemer and Nora Fok or the finely observed twig forms that give structure to Cynthia Cousens's necklaces. These non-linear forms reflect a new understanding of the underlying order of the natural world. Mandelbrot himself noted: "Our graphics [fractals] did more than inform. They made people dream."[5]

Susan Enterline, Svenja John, Maria Phillips, and Maria Hanson all explore geometric forms that lie somewhere between those of nature and those described by the constructs of mathematics.[6] In some respects, the jewelry of these artists parallels the work of contemporary architects whose structures reflect changing views of nature. Frank Gehry's Guggenheim Museum in Bilbao, Peter Eisenman's Aronoff Center in Cincinnati, and Daniel Libeskind's Jewish Museum in Berlin can all be appreciated as reflections of a post-Newtonian view of the universe that demands a new way of seeing, a new language, and new metaphors.[7]

Whether or not the artists in *Hanging in Balance* consciously attempted to depict a new world view, the sophistication with which they interpreted nature is in accord with our changing understanding of the world. In going beyond the arcane language of mathematics to give form to its underlying insights, they help us make sense out of complex natural phenomena[8] and give new meaning to Aristotle's observation, "Art partly completes what nature cannot bring to finish and partly imitates her."[9]

In considering the degree to which artistic images reflect our changing worldview, it is interesting to consider whether the free-form works of Sandra Enterline and Maria Hanson, the wild geometries of plastic polycarbonate in the hands of Svenja John, the cascading circlets of Helen Dorion, the organic forms of Maria Phillips, or the fine filaments of Cynthia Cousens could have been considered valid, let alone exciting, jewelry pieces just a few decades ago.

While focusing on the contemporary aspects of the neckpieces in *Hanging in Balance*, it is equally important to recognize that these cutting-edge statements are part of a continuum that extends back tens of thousands of years. The earliest jewelry, dating from 30,000 B.C., was based on natural forms and local materials[10] and embodied a spirituality tied to fertility and survival that reflected an intimate relationship with the natural world. Contemporary jewelry, to the degree that it expresses ideas related to the inbuilt energy of our surroundings, can be linked to the power that resonates in the jewelry of early cultures and that still resides in the body ornaments of many non-Western societies today. As Swiss painter Paul Klee stated, "This thing we call nature is not merely physical reality; it is also — at least for those who have creative aspirations — the revelation of a mysterious inner life."[11]

The sophisticated and expressive necklaces in *Hanging in Balance* are deeply felt and masterfully realized artistic visions. Rooted in the artists' passion for life, their devotion to the human body, and their sensitivity to the forces of the natural world, they express complex relationships and insights, both conceptual and aesthetic, in wearable form.

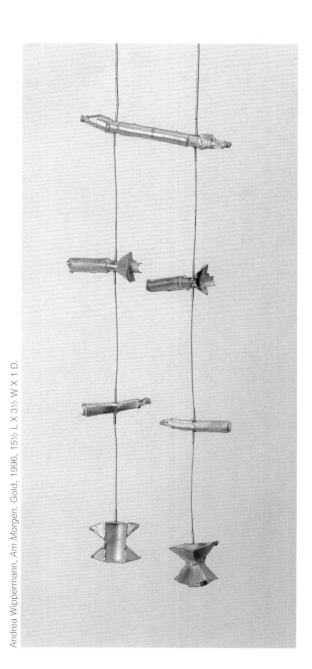

Andrea Wippermann, *Am Morgen*. Gold, 1996, 15½ L X 3½ W X 1 D.

[1] The movement against precious materials was led by Dutch jewelers during a highly inventive period from 1965 to the early 1970s.

[2] The plumb bob is one of the oldest tools in the world, dating back to around 2600 B.C., when the Egyptians used it for building. It is simply a cord with a weight suspended from it that responds to gravitational attraction by pointing toward the earth's center of gravity.

[3] In contemporary jewelry, large, sculptural neck collars can be traced to the theatrical neckpieces of Gijs Bakker and Emmy van Leersum in the 1960s. These works required the use of lightweight materials, principally aluminum, and reflected the artists' ambition to work as sculptors for the human body.

[4] The tradition is ancient; in the thirteenth century Fibonacci uncovered the mathematical relationship known as the golden ratio that appear in works as diverse as the Egyptian pyramids and the paintings of Renaissance masters.

[5] Benoit Mandelbrot, foreword to Michael McGuire, *An Eye for Fractals* (Reading, Mass.: Addison-Wesley Publishing Company, 1991).

[6] Patricia Harris and David Lyon, "Mystery and Memory: The Jewelry of Sandra Enterline," *Metalsmith 24* (Spring 2004): 30–39.

[7] Charles Jencks, "Nonlinear Architecture: New Science = New Architecture?" in *Architectural Design*, no. 129 1997, 69.

[8] Oscar Wilde took the extreme view that our knowledge of nature was entirely a result of the creation of art: "Nature is no great mother who has borne us. She is our creation." Oscar Wilde, "The Influence of the Impressionists On Climate," in *The Selected Prose of Oscar Wilde*, Project Gutenberg Release #1338 (June 1998), onlinebooks. library.upenn.edu.

[9] Aristotle *Physics, Book II* (London, Oxford University Press, 1999), 242.

[10] One of the earliest necklaces from the Paleolithic Era, found in the Czech Republic and dating from ca. 28,000 B.C., was made of fossilized shell beads, but others contained carved bones, fish vertebrae, animal teeth, claws, stone beads, and healing herbs. Daniella Mascetti and Amanda Triossi, *The Necklace from Antiquity to the Present* (New York: Harry N. Abrams, 1997), 9.

[11] Carola Giedion-Weicker, *Paul Klee* (New York: Faber and Faber, 1952), 52.

Hanging in Balance
Kate Bonansinga

During the late incubation period of this exhibition, after the artists had been invited and the title secured, I listened to a compact disk of Don DeLillo's *The Body Artist*, read by performance artist Laurie Anderson. The first quarter of this spare novella is the story of a couple's morning routine: preparing and eating breakfast, listening to the radio and reading the newspaper. The husband's obituary directly follows this scene, so we learn that it was actually the couple's last meal together. The rest of the story covers several months of the widow coping with her husband's death, her grief, resolve, and ultimate transformation.

This story and its title still haunt me. Our bodies are our most tangible tool for experiencing life, as opposed to, for example, our spirits or our minds. Similarly, the art object is a tangible catalyst for feelings and ideas. By bringing "body" and "artist" together, DeLillo connects the physicality of the object with the ephemeralness of the art experience. His main character, the widow, is, like Anderson, a performance artist who employs her body alone for artistic expression. Here Anderson conveys an intimate understanding of a fellow performer's worldview. Her expressive portrayal of the widow's reality connects it to the listener's own, and we experience the widow's relativity of time and emotion and her confusion of loss. The personal (hers) becomes universal (ours), the tangible (body) becomes ethereal (art), and the common becomes transcendent.

The relationship between the necklaces exhibited here and DeLillo's character goes beyond the their shared emphasis on the human body. There are four parties involved in the experience of both necklace and character-portrayed-aloud: the creator, the created, the interpreter (i.e., the wearer of the necklace and the reader (Laurie Anderson) of the novella), and the audience. The interpreter dramatically affects the experience of the audience, and this direct and obvious interpretive act is typically absent in the fine art triumvirate of artist/art/viewer. Thus, a necklace being worn is more akin to an actor performing than it is to a static work of art, because the wearer's stance and movement impacts the piece and brings it to life.

This influence is mutual. Each of the necklaces exhibited here affects how the wearer interacts with her surrounding world. Some shape the wearer's posture, some are weighty, some are extraordinarily long, some create sound, and yet others are defined by their fragility. To wear them requires a high level of consciousness on the part of the wearer. They go beyond the role of traditional jewelry as a decorative emblem of status, and force the wearer to be present in her body and take notice of herself. Additionally, each of these neckpieces addresses a larger theme, one that it communicates whether it is being worn or not.

Repetition and Delicacy

Helen Ellison-Dorion links together small hoops of fine and sterling silver to create dense assemblages. The relationship of the hoops is not mathematically determined, but there is never the less a sense of underlying order. In *Untitled #1*, the compilation of hoops covers the entire chest, like a heavy bib or an undergarment for armor. Though the individual parts are delicate, together they create a strong, protective layer: the neckpiece is a mediator between the wearer and her surrounding world. Distributed randomly amongst the silver elements are tiny, enameled flowers, which seem to struggle to burst forth from the overlay of hoops that both connects and represses them. Circles symbolize eternity, continuity and cycles. Here they connect with each other and then surround the neck: circles encircle, doubling the impact of their symbolism.

In *Untitled #2* Dorion's silver hoops link together to create a hefty three-dimensional line, punctuated at each end by a dense cluster of loops interspersed with flat, rusty-red enamel ellipses.Its format lends it the versatility of a scarf or a boa: the wearer can drape it around her neck so that the clusters rest on either her chest or her back, swinging like perfectly balanced pendulums, side by side. Or she can tightly wind *Untitled #2* so that it becomes a silver collar, and the negative spaces between the loops in effect disappear. Dorion began her career as a textile artist, a history evident in her linked and woven metal forms.

In **Nora Fok**'s *The Flower of Love* a circle of thick, metal wire rests on the wearer's shoulders. Suspended from this support are yellow nylon threads, tipped pink at their ends. They cover the chest, shoulders and back with the density of a mane, but the title indicates a floral, rather than animal, source of inspiration. If this is the case, the wearer's head becomes a stamen, her body a stem, the neckpiece the flower's variegated petals. Its softness and tactility invite caress, but its density and form suggest protection.

Hanging in Balance also drapes the shoulders and, thus, completely changes compositionally if the wearer raises her arms. Interlaced lines of nylon suspend multiple and evenly spaced acrylic balls, which the artist likens to dew drops on a spider's web. They can also reference sources of light, such as Asian paper lanterns, strung up

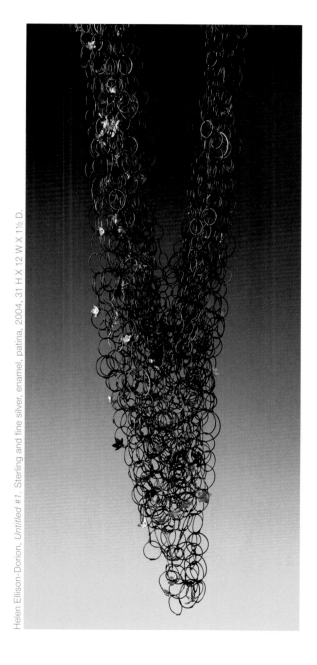

Helen Ellison-Dorion, *Untitled #1*. Sterling and fine silver, enamel, patina, 2004, 31 H X 12 W X 1½ D.

Nora Fok, *Looping Waves*, detail. Nylon, 2004, 13¾ Diameter overall.

in celebration, or stars in the night sky. Just as the twenty-eight-day schedule of the moon and rotation of the earth determine the annual rhythm of the constellations and their visibility to earth-bound observers, the movement of the wearer's torso and arms impact the relationship between Fok's star-like dewdrops. The wearer is the decisive force.

Looping Waves is most similar to Fok's previous pectorals and is inspired by the starched collars of the Renaissance and Baroque periods, fashionable symbols of social and financial status. True to its title, it can also be likened to ocean waves, the patterned loops of monofilament forming larger and more complex loops that extend away from the body, stiffening into the third dimension.

Flatness made Dimensional

Bettina Dittlmann draws in metal, bending thin wire into forms that resemble outlines of floral patterns. She maintains a spontaneity and freeness that encourages the eye to move around the entire design, regardless of whether it is on or off the body. It also connects these works to the lineage of automatic drawing established by the Surrealists of the early twentieth century. These necklaces maintain the childlike and immediate appeal of the flat, colorful enamel pendants that comprised the artist's previous body of work.

Svenja John's pendants look like futuristic architectural models or abstractions of engineered flora and fauna. The artist cuts flat pieces of Makrolon (a high-tech plastic widely used to manufacture CDs, DVDs, sports eyewear, golf tees and solar panels, amongst other consumer goods) or Macrofol (a polycarbonate film) into pleasing, abstract shapes. She then layers them to create a three-dimensional form, its interior a series of cavities created by planes that abut and connect, often by means of barbell-shaped tabs inserted into perforations in the plastic or polycarbonate.

Sometimes the planes are hand-colored by the artist and outlined in black so that they maintain an individual presence. But they also combine with ease to create a volumetric entity; the colors seem to change with the amount and intensity of the light and the viewing angle. In material, method and form, these works presage the future, windows on things to come.

At the beginning of her professional career **Jan Baum** created lockets with multiple chambers, often filled with organic matter. In the late 1990s the artist simplified and flattened her forms, layering them and adding bright colors and patterns. The necklaces presented here are inspired by facial tattoos on the Maori people of New Zealand and are her most graphic and linear works to date. They consist of lines of steel bent into flat shapes that resemble images from nature, such as clouds and birds. Each image rests on the upper chest and is readable immediately and from a distance, almost like signage.

Considered Rawness

Iris Bodemer utilizes myriad materials to project a considered rawness in each of her works. In *No. 04-002*, for example, three bronze forms shaped like shields are connected together, their upper edge creating a continuous horizon line. Suspended above each shield is a complementary element: at the left is a smooth, flat, oval pebble; in the center a string of garnet beads coiled into a pile; and to the right a grid of four squares of wool. Bodemer employs units of threes and fours that multiply to twelve, referencing months of the year and hours in half of a day and, consequently, the larger issue of the passage of time. Attached to the leftmost bronze element is a bundle of red wool; to the right a is rough-cut gem framed in wool thread; and centered are four garnet tear drops, the deep red of blood, bold counterpoints to the string of beads hovering, like the sun, directly above.

This reference to landscape continues in *No. 04-015*, comprised of a piece of earth-colored rubber, shaped like a papoose swaddled in a blanket decorated with a grid of rectangular, uncultured pearls. Hanging in context on the body, it is taller than it is wide and is large enough to completely cover the chest, like a protective bib. Bodemer turns it on its side when displaying it off of the body, literally laying it down and putting it to rest. On the body, *No. 04-015* is a figure; off the body, it is a landscape. Thus, the artist accentuates the decontextualization of the work when it is off the body, rather than attempting to replicate the manner in which the jewelry responds to the human form.

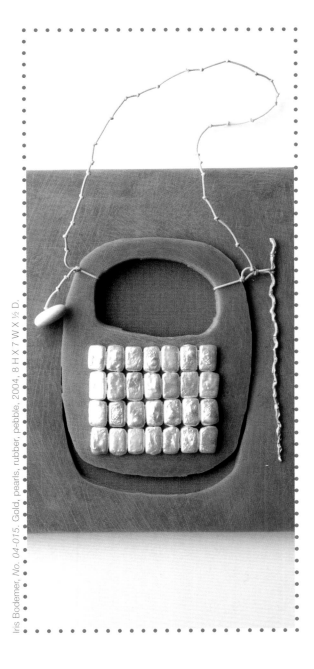

Iris Bodemer, *No. 04-015*. Gold, pearls, rubber, pebble, 2004, 8 H X 7 W X ½ D.

No. 04-001, like *No. 04-015,* changes dramatically when it rests on a horizontal surface. Then, four metal cylinders, each about the size of a teacup, serve as containers, one for each of the four major elements of the necklace. The containers are the visual focal point and almost entirely obscure their contents, lending them an air of secrecy. In contrast, when worn, strung quartz beads drape around the neck, suspending a bundle of wool and some twigs on one side, a cylinder of bone with a bronze backdrop on the other. In shape and proportion, the bundles reference sculpture, the bronze rectangle references painting. One balances the other.

Much like Bodemer, **Andrea Wippermann**'s coarse aesthetic conveys sophisticated refinement. Her work seems to be continuously in progress, as if resolution is antithetical to the journey of discovery. In *Frösche,* four gold elements shaped like W's share an abstracted anthropomorphism; their outermost segments look like arms or legs. The nylon string that suspends them also connects the two inner segments on each element, and each element to the next. Thus, each "torso" is tied to the other three torsos, creating a group dynamic. *Am Morgen* also establishes relationships, but between cast gold elements that look like tiny bundles, their contents a mystery

For the past few years, **Maria Phillips** has created organs and pods from animal gut and the works in *Hanging in Balance* continue in that vein. In *Flush,* four groups of pale pods hang together, descending from smallest to largest. These allusions to incipient life and growth hang on one side of the body, balanced on the other side by a single element that has the skeletal shape of a dandelion blossom after it has shed its petals. Thus, death counteracts life. In *Accumulate* Phillips casts resin in the shape of feet to encapsulate discarded matter, both organic and inorganic, from her domestic environment. Remnants of the artist's world have resettled in these replicas of the human body part that is most often in contact with the earth. By suspending these connectors of land and body at waist level, Phillips elevates them both physically and metaphorically.

Restriction

Anika Smulovitz deconstructs and amends the collars of men's white dress shirts to be women's neckpieces. The collars are rigid, references to the rigidity of our social hierarchy and the lifestyles of the starched-collared, male inhabitants of the upper levels of that hierarchy. By literally tearing apart this symbol of privilege and power, Smulovitz advocates that in today's world of Internet millionaires and increased social mobility through education, creativity and hard work, this hierarchy is irrelevant.

For many of the pieces the artist removes the collar entirely; for others the collar remains connected to portions of the original shirt, which, in turn, mask portions of the wearer's torso, like intentionally inadequate and seductive clothing. In the words of the artist, "Why is it that, when removed from the shirt, white collars are considered sexy, bringing to mind Playboy bunnies?"[1] These collars have neither the preciousness of traditional jewelry nor the function of traditional clothing, yet they draw upon associations with both, and twist assumptions about class, wealth and gender.

Maru Almeida has an ongoing fascination with jewelry's "closeness to our senses and interaction with our body."[2] *Felt Formations I-III* combine tubular, branch-like felt formations into pectorals that blanket the upper chest. Within these tactile forms are magnets, literal and metaphorical attractors and connectors, not only between the jewelry and the wearer,

but also between the wearer and other aspects of her world. In the past Almeida has employed dyed sugar as ephemeral body adornment in a comment on the beauty and transience of life. With these newest works in felt, she offers permanence, warmth, and sustenance during a time of domestic and international uncertainty.

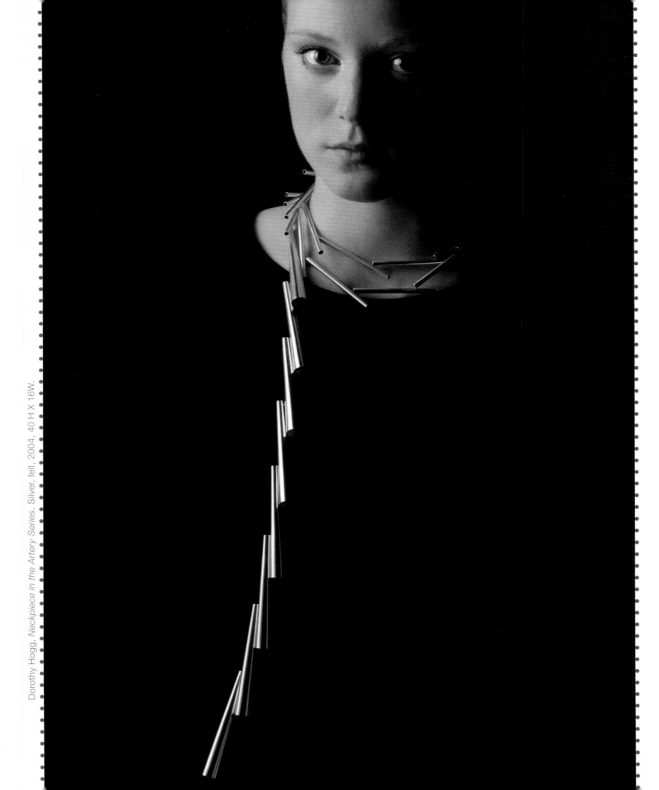

Containment

Whereas Almeida is new to the art jewelry scene, **Dorothy Hogg** has been creating jewelry for decades. She works primarily in silver and gold, but recently has added felt and coral to offer a splash of color that references blood. And though *Neckpiece from the Artery Series* resembles a blood vessel, it can also be likened to a spine.

The references in Hogg's work go beyond the human body. The artist credits the seascape of her hometown of Troon, on the west coast of Scotland, as a fundamental source, stating: "...transient skies of every tone of grey with dark islands and headlands juxtaposed against a silvery changing sea. My eye is so attuned to these subtle and monochromatic tones that this has resulted in a tendency in my work to be restrained and understated."[3] Her medium is precious metals, and she steadfastly resisted trends in the 1970s and 1980s to create from alternative materials. However, the method in which her works embrace and hang from the body is far from traditional. In her *Tumbling Necklace*, one side balances the other, with symmetrical precision. Four diminutive vessel shapes, two on each side of the body, hang from silver chains, and emit elegant silver outlines that reference pouring liquid. When these silver forms come together, they produce a soft sound, like a murmur. Hogg has consistently experimented with kinetic and aural effects, patterns of light and surface textures, minimal detail and a restrained palette. One critic described her *Dispersal Necklace* from 2000 as having "the geometric endless column of Brancusi."[4]

Sandra Enterline and Hogg explore similar themes in their work and share an interest in elegant form and muted tones. Enterline states that her

Sandra Enterline, *Untitled*, detail. Pearls, oxidized sterling, rubies, stainless steel, 2004, hanging length: 23.

Maria Hanson, *Interlock #1*, detail. Oxidized silver, gold leaf, black ribbon, 1994, hanging length: 40 1/3.

"jewelry explores human ideas at an appropriately human scale. In materials that range from butter-flies' wings to rubies, pieces exploit such physical qualities of form as front/back and exterior/interior to question concepts of the precious, the memorable, the familiar and the strange. It creates a connection between the body and the world and becomes a sensuous amulet against the ideational remoteness of modern life."[5] Her best-known pendants have the form of containers and seem to hold secrets to the past, like a traditional locket holding physical remnants of loved ones and the deceased, symbols of their memory. But they also point to the future, with their streamline and aerodynamic aesthetic. Enterline often perforates her forms, as if the contents of the interior need to breathe and as if we, as viewers, need a tiny bit of access to the inaccessible.

Maria Hanson shares Enterline's interest in perforation, but the forms in *Interlock #1* and *Interlock #2* are more organic than those of Enterline. Many of Hanson's works look like austere cages, but these pieces reference cohabitation rather than confinement. In both *Interlock #1* and *Interlock #2* Hanson slips misshapen forms through flat disks. The placement of the elements on the body and in relationship to one another depends upon how tightly the cable hugs the neck. The archaic definition of "depend" is "to hang down or be suspended from something." Hanson's work conveys both the contemporary and earlier meanings of the word.

My premonition that the themes addressed in Don DeLillo's *The Body Artist* connect somehow to those addressed by the necklaces exhibited here led me to learn more about the author and his place in contemporary fiction. One literary critic, Jesse Kavadlo, based an entire volume on exploring

"DeLillo's use of balance — as a trope within the novels, and as a self-conscious expression of the author's place in the world. The novels themselves help to balance, or counterbalance, the conditions of the world that they illustrate."[6]

This may also be said of this group of necklaces. They require their wearers to stand and sit up straight, to go forward in the world with confidence and poise, to maintain a sense of equilibrium, even if the society and culture that surrounds them seems to be loosing its center. Though none of the artists intends didacticism or even narrative, when considered in this context the works achieve a broader social message. They hang in balance and require us to do so, as well.

This emphasis on the potential of the individual to initiate change, to use her physical being to adjust her surroundings and how she interacts with them, exemplifies a step beyond postmodernism and into a post-9/11 world, when skepticism is, by necessity, vanquished by the belief that recovery is possible. Under the best circumstances, both readers and listeners of *The Body Artist* become immersed in the widow's reality to the point that it balances their own. If the wearers connect with these necklaces, the results may be the same.

[1]As quoted from the artist's statement, 2004.

[2]As quoted from the artist's statement, 2004.

[3]As quoted in Shannon Tofts, "Sources of Inspiration: Dorothy Hogg." In *Crafts* (May/June 2000): 48-51.

[4]Marina Vaizey, "Dorothy Hogg-Jeweller." In *Dorothy Hogg: Ten Year Retrospective, 1994-2004* (Edinburgh: The Scottish Gallery, 2004), unpaginated.

[5]As quoted from the artist's statement, 2003.

[6]Jesse Kavadlo, *Don DeLillo: Balance on the Edge of Belief* (New York: Peter Lang, 2004), 10.

Maru Almeida, *Formation II, Crystals*. Hand-felted wool, 2004, 7 Diameter.

Maru Almeida

(b. 1974, Durango, Mexico; resides, Seattle, WA)

Education
2002   M.F.A., University of Oregon
1998   B.F.A., University of Texas at El Paso

Select Recent Exhibitions
Group
2004   *3D: Devilish, Decadent, Delicious*, Emely Davis Gallery, Akron, OH
2003   *Taste and Bytes*, The Other Gallery, Banff, Alberta, Canada

Awards
2003   The Banff Centre Artistic Scholarship, The Banff Centre

Jan Baum

(b. 1966, Doylestown, PA; resides Towson, MD)

Education
1994   M.F.A., University of Massachusetts Dartmouth
1988   B.F.A., Arcadia University, Glenside, PA

Selected Recent Exhibitions
Group
2004   *Two Capitals: Contemporary Jewelry*, The Museum of Decorative and Applied Arts, Moscow
2003   *Enamel: A Current Perspective, Exhibition in Print*, *Metalsmith* and *SOFA Chicago*, Chicago, IL
2003   *Craft Transformed: PIA at the Swain School, 1985-1987, University of Massachusetts Dartmouth
        1998 to the present*, University Art Gallery, New Bedford, MA

Awards
1999   Travel Grant, Oregon College of Art and Craft, Portland, Oregon

Collections
Renwick Gallery, National Museum of American Art at the Smithsonian Institution
Oregon College of Art and Craft
L.A. Eyeworks

Jan Baum, *Tattoo #1 (Maori #1)*, Steel, silver, 2004, form only: 1¾ H X 2⅛ W.

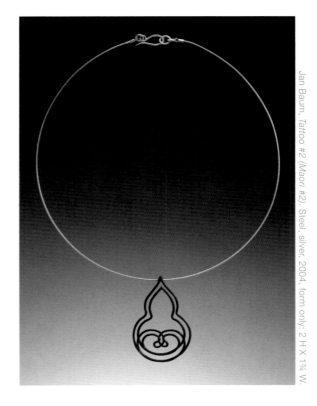

Jan Baum, *Tattoo #2 (Maori #2)*, Steel, silver, 2004, form only: 2 H X 1¾ W.

Jan Baum, *Bird (Tattoo # 4)*, Steel, silver, 2004, form only: 1⅜ H X 2 W.

Iris Bodemer, *No 04-002*. Bronze, diamond crystal, onyx, garnet, wool, 2004, 10 H X 6 W X ⅓ D.

Iris Bodemer

(b. 1970, Paderborn, Germany; resides Pforzheim, Germany)

Education

1997   M.A., Sandberg Institute, Amsterdam
1996   Diploma, Fachhochschule fur Gestaltung, Pforzheim
1989-92 Apprenticeship, Goldsmith's School, Pforzheim

Selected Recent Exhibitions
Solo
2004   Jewelers'werk Galerie, Washington, DC
2002   Galerie Marzee, Nijmegen, The Netherlands
2001   Tactile, Geneva
2000   Galerie Marzee, Nijmegen, The Netherlands
Group
2003   *Valuables: Jewelry in the New Millennium*, Museum of Craft and Folk Art, San Francisco, CA
2002   *Pièce à Conviction*, Tactile, Geneva
2002   *Extrakt*, Bauhaus-Archiv/Museum für Gestaltung, Berlin

Awards
2002   Schöner Verlag Königsbach-Stein
2001   *Marzeepreis*, Galerie Marzee, Nijmegen, The Netherlands

Collections
Stedelijk Museum, Amsterdam
Museum Voor Moderne Kunst, Arnhem, The Netherlands
Schmuckmuseum, Pforzheim

Cynthia Cousens

(b. 1956, Ipswich, England; resides East Sussex, England)

Education
1982   M.A., Royal College of Art
1978   B.A., Loughborough College of Art and Design

Select Recent Exhibitions
Solo
2003   Hove Museum ACE National Touring Programme, Brighton, England
1999   Crafts Council Shop at the Victoria and Albert Museum, London
1998   Hipotesi, Barcelona
Group
2000   *Jerwood Prize for Applied Arts Exhibition*, Crafts Council and traveling
1998   *Jewellery Moves*, National Museums of Scotland, Edinburgh
1998   *Beyond Material*, Oriel Mostyn Llandudno and traveling

Awards
1995 & 2000 Shortlist for *Jerwood Prize for Applied Arts*, *Jewellery*, United Kingdom

Collections
Victoria and Albert Museum
National Museums of Scotland
Musee de L'Hologerie Geneva

Cynthia Cousens, *Blue Tint*, detail. Acetate, monofilament, 2004, 33½ H X 35½ W X ⅓ D overall.

40

Bettina Dittlmann

(b.1964, Passau, Germany; resides Berlin, Germany)

Education
1991   M.A., State University of New York, New Paltz
1993   Diploma, Academy of Fine Art, Munich, Germany

Selected Recent Exhibitions
Solo
2003   Galleri hnoss, Göteborg, Sweden
2002   *Centonzecercles*, Galerie Hélèn Poreè, Paris
2002   Galerie vice-versa, Lausanne, Switzerland
Group
2004   Galerie Hélèn Poreé at *COLLECT*, Victoria and Albert Museum, London
2003   Jewelers'werk Galerie at *SOFA New York*, New York, NY
2003   *Dannerpreis* 2002, Museum of Applied Arts, Prague
2001   *Micromegas*, Bayrischer Kunstgewerbeverein, Munich

Awards
2003   *Landespreis* of the City of Berlin, Anerkennung
2001   *Herbert-Hofmann-Preis*, Handwerksmesse, Munich
1999   *Prinzregent-Luitpold-Stiftung*, Munich

Bettina Dittlmann, *Flowers*. Iron, silver solder, 2004, 15 H X 12 W.

Helen Ellison-Dorion, *Untitled* #2. Sterling and fine silver, enamel, patina, 2004, 72 H (extended).

Helen Ellison-Dorion

(b. 1965, Bolton, England; resides El Paso, Texas)

Education
1998   M.A. University of Texas at El Paso
1987   B.A. The Sir John Moores University, Liverpool, England

Recent Exhibitions
Group
2004   *Blue*, Mobilia Gallery, Cambridge, MA
2003   *Botanical Jewelry*, Mobilia Gallery, Cambridge, MA and *SOFA Chicago*, Chicago, IL
2003   *Art for the Ear*, Mobilia Gallery, Cambridge, MA and *SOFA New York*, New York, NY
2003   *The Teapot Redefined*, Mobilia Gallery, Cambridge, MA, and *SOFA Chicago*, Chicago, IL
2002   *The Teapot Redefined*, Mobilia Gallery, Cambridge, MA, and *SOFA Chicago*, Chicago, IL
1999   *USA Craft Today 99*, Third Juried Biennial, Silvermine Guild Arts Centre, New Canaan, CT

Sandra Enterline

(b. 1960 in Oil City, PA; resides San Francisco, CA)

Education
1983   B.F.A., Rhode Island School of Design, Providence, RI
1980   Associate Degree, Rochester Institute of Technology,
        School for American Craftsmen, Rochester, NY

Selected Recent Exhibitions
Solo
1999   *One Thousand Souvenirs*, Susan Cummins Gallery, Mill Valley, CA
1996   *Breaking Ground*, Susan Cummins Gallery, Mill Valley, CA
1989   Rezac Gallery, Chicago, IL
1989   Jewelers'werk Galerie, Washington, D.C.

Group
2004   *RISD Faculty & Alumni Show*, Galerie Marzee, Nijmegen, The Netherlands
2004   *Crocker Kingsley 73rd Exhibition*, Crocker Art Museum, Sacramento, CA
2003   *Valuables: Jewelry in the New Millennium*, Museum of Craft & Folk Art, San Francisco, CA

Collections
Museum of Arts and Design
Oakland Museum of Art
Renwick Gallery, National Museum of American Art at the Smithsonian Institution

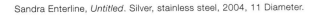

Sandra Enterline, *Untitled*. Silver, stainless steel, 2004, 11 Diameter.

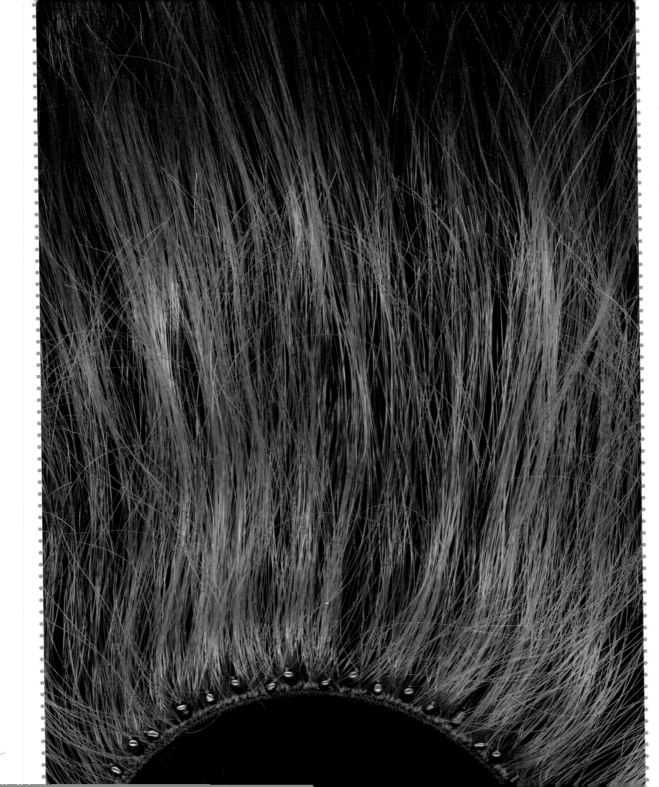

48

Nora Fok

(b. 1953, Hong Kong; resides East Sussex, England)

Education
1981   B.A., Brighton Polytechnic University, Brighton, England
1977   Higher Certificate, Hong Kong Polytechnic University, Kowloon, Hong Kong
1972   Centre Certificate, Kwan Tong Vocational Training Center, Kowloon, Hong Kong

Selected Recent Exhibitions
Solo
1999   *Galaxies*, The Pearoom, Heckington, England and Hove Museum and Art Gallery, East Sussex, England
Group
2004   British Crafts Council at *SOFA Chicago*, Chicago, IL
2004   *Weaving Stories*, Low Parks Museum, Hamilton, Scotland
2004   Body Conscious, Crafts Council Shop at the Victoris and Albert Museum, London
2003   *Jewelry Hard and Soft*, The Society of Arts and Crafts, Boston, MA
2003   *Jewelry Meets Textile*, Contemporary Applied Arts, London
2002   British Crafts Council at *SOFA Chicago*, Chicago, IL
2002   *Material Explorations*, The Munson Williams Proctor Arts Institute School of Art, Utica, NY
2001   Mobilia Gallery at *SOFA Chicago*, Chicago, IL and *SOFA New York*, New York, NY

Selected Collections
National Museums of Scotland
Museum fur Kunst und Gewerbe, Hamburg
City of Bristol Museum and Art Gallery

Nora Fok, *Flower of Love*, detail. Nylon, black pearls, 2004, 27½ Diameter.

Maria Hanson

(b. 1967 Yorkshire, England; resides, Sheffield, England

Education
1991   M.A., Royal College of Art, London, England
1989   B.A., West Surrey College of Art and Design, Farnham, Surrey, England

Selected Recent Exhibitions
Solo
1999   DESIGNyard, Dublin
1998   The School of Jewellery, Birmingham, England
1998   The Scottish Gallery, Edinburgh, Scotland
Group
2003   *CHESS*, traveling, U.S.A. and U.K.
2003   *Showcase Exhibition*, Crafts Council Shop at the Victoria and Albert Museum, London
2002   *B1 3PA*, Gallerie Metallum, Stockholm

Awards
2000   Shortlist for *Jerwood Prize for Applied Arts, Jewellery*, United Kingdom
1997/98/99 *Research Award*, University of Central England
1997   *Individual Artist's Award*, Yorkshire and Humberside Arts

Collections
Yorkshire Artspace Society
Birmingham Museum and Art Gallery
Crafts Council Collection

Maria Hanson, *Interlock #2 (Neckpiece)*. Silver, gold leaf and blue ribbon, 1994, hanging length: 35 ½.

Dorothy Hogg

(b. 1945 Troon, Scotland; resides in Edinburgh, Scotland)

Education
1972   Certificate of Education, Moray House College of Education
1970   Master of Design, Royal College of Art
1968   Diploma of Art, Glasgow School of Art

Selected Recent Exhibitions
Solo
2004   *Dorothy Hogg: Ten Year Retrospective, 1994-2004*, The Scottish Gallery, Edinburgh, Scotland
Group
2004   The Scottish Gallery at *COLLECT*, Victoria and Albert Museum, London
2003   *Koru, Selected Exhibition of European Makers*, Finland
2003   *CHESS*, traveling, U.S.A. and U.K.
2002   *Schmuck 2002*, IHM, Munich
2002   The Scottish Gallery at *SOFA Chicago*, Chicago, IL
2001   *The Ring*, Mobilia Gallery, Cambridge, MA and traveling

Honors and Awards
2001   MBE for services to Jewellery and Silversmithing
2000   Shortlist for *Jerwood Prize for Applied Arts, Jewellery,* England
1977   *Lilly McDougall Award*, Scottish Society of Women Artists
1977   *Ian Clarkson Competition*, England

Collections
Musee des Arts Decoratifs, Montreal
National Museums of Scotland
The Crafts Council, London

Svenja John

(b. 1963, Duisburg, West Germany; resides Berlin, Germany)

Education
1993   Master's Diploma, State Academy, Hanau, Germany
1991   Degree, Goldsmith's School, Hanau, Germany
1989   Degree, Ruhr University, Bochum, Germany

Selected Recent Exhibitions
Solo
2004   *Polycolometron*, Galerie Aurum, Frankfurt, Germany
2003   *Transparenz 10*, Museum für Angewandte Kunst Köln, Köln, Germany
2003   *Tube*, Jewelers'werk Galerie, Washington, DC
Group
2004   *Kunst Rai*, Galerie Ra, Amsterdam
2004   *Schmuck 2004*, IHM, Munich
2004   *Loot!*, Museum of Arts and Design, New York

Awards
2004   *Herbert-Hofmann-Preis*, IHM, Munich
2000   *Bayerischer Staatspreis*, Munich
1999   *Landespreis*, Berlin

Collections
Kunstgewerbemuseum
Grassi Museum
Museum of Arts and Design

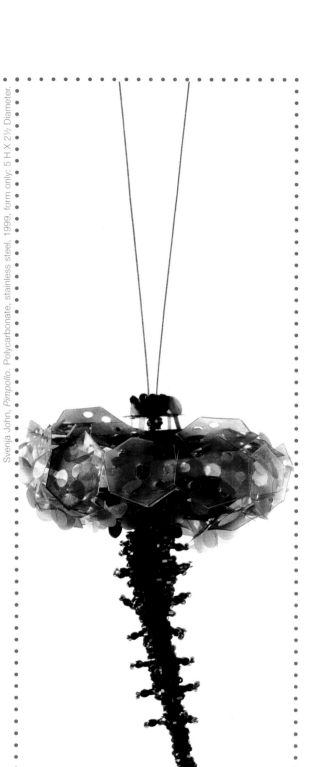

Svenja John, *Pimpollo*, Polycarbonate, stainless steel, 1999, form only: 5 H X 2½ Diameter.

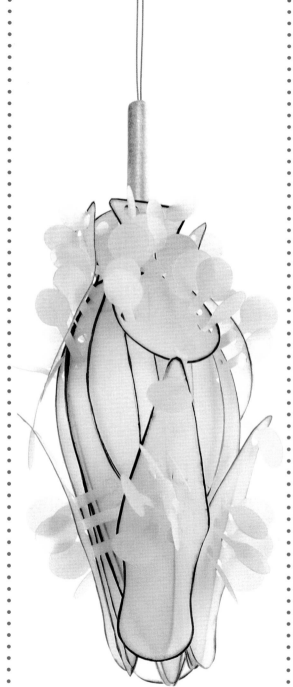

Svenja John, *Semilla*, Polycarbonate, stainless steel, 2000, form only: 4 H X 1¼ Diameter.

Maria Phillips. *Parturiant*, detail. Plaster, steel, gut, gold plated silver, silver, 2004. 22 H X 11 W X 1 D overall.

Maria Phillips
(b. 1963, St. Louis, MO; resides, Seattle, WA)

Education
1997   M.F.A., University of Washington, Seattle, WA
1986   B.A., Loyola University, New Orleans, LA

Selected Recent Exhibitions
Solo
2002   Susan Cummins Gallery, Mill Valley, CA
2000   Susan Cummins Gallery, Mill Valley, CA
1999   Susan Cummins Gallery, Mill Valley, CA
Group
2004   *COLLECT*, Victoria and Albert Museum, London
2004   *Current Directions: Studio Art Jewelry*, Delaware Center for the Contemporary Arts, Wilmington, DE
2003   *Evocative Objects*, Bannister Gallery, Rhode Island College, Providence, RI

Awards
2003   Artist Trust/Washington State Arts Commission Fellowship
2002   Merit Award, Craftsman's Choice, Smithsonian Craft Show
2001   American Craft Emerging Artist Grant

Collections
John Michael Kohler Arts Center
Tacoma Art Museum

Anika Smulovitz

(b. 1974, Phoenix, AZ; resides, Boise, ID)

Education
2003   M.F.A., University of Wisconsin, Madison, WI
2001   M.A., University of Wisconsin, Madison, WI
1997   B.F.A., University of Oregon, Eugene, OR

Selected Recent Exhibitions
Solo
2005 East Central College Gallery, East Central College, Union, MO
2004 DeLuce Gallery, Northwest Missouri State University, Maryville, MO
Group
2004 *Elements of 5: 5th Year Anniversary Exhibition*, Sculpture to Wear, Santa Monica, CA
2004 *Visiting Artist Exhibition*, Interlochen Arts Academy, Interlochen, MI
2003 *Evocative Objects*, Bannister Gallery, Rhode Island College, Providence, RI

Awards
2002 *New American Craft Award of Merit*, Concord Art Association, MA

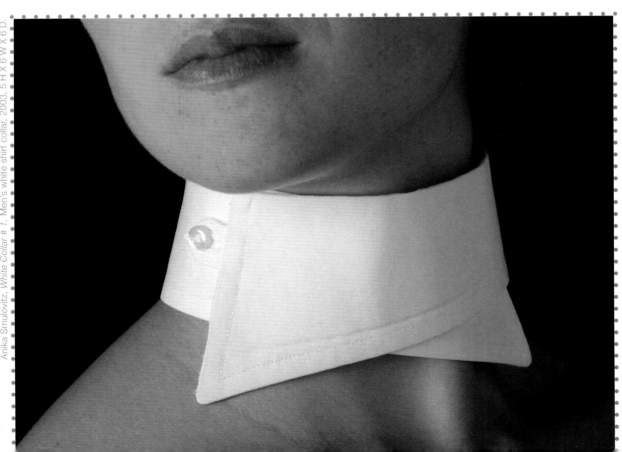

Anika Smulovitz, *White Collar # 1*. Men's white shirt collar, 2003, 5 H X 6 W X 6 D.

58

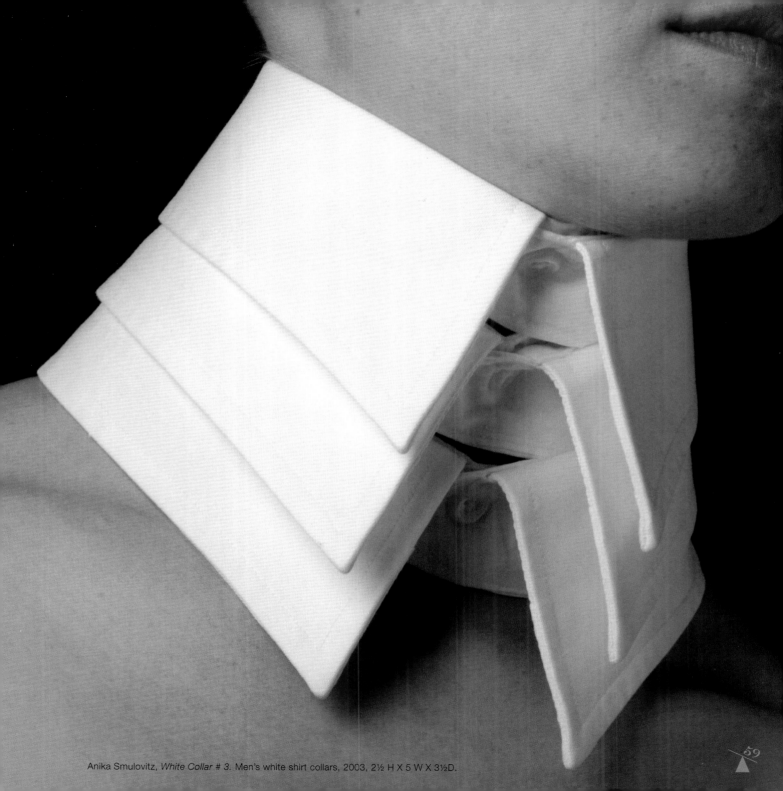

Anika Smulovitz, *White Collar # 3.* Men's white shirt collars, 2003, 2½ H X 5 W X 3½D.

Andrea Wippermann
(b. 1963, Rostock, East Germany; resides Halle, Germany)

Education
1992-3 Postgraduate Study, School for Art and Design, Halle
1991   Degree, School for Art and Design, Halle

Selected Recent Exhibitions
Solo
2003   Jewelers'werk Galerie,Washington, D.C.
2003   Galerie Marzee, Nijmegen, The Netherlands
Group
2002   *Der Dinge Heimlich Leben- das erzählerische Moment im Schmuck*,
        Galerie Marktschloß chen, Halle, Kloster Unser lieben Fraun in Magdeburg
2002   *Sommerfestival, Internationale Schmuckkunst*, Galerie Slavik, Wien
2002   *Schmuck 2002*, IHM, Munich

Awards
1998   Herbert Hofmann Prize, Munich
1996   Bursary from the Kunsthaus Gutenberg, Ahrenshoop

Collections
Staatliche Galerie Moritzburg, Halle
The Kunstgewerbemuseum, Pforzheim
The Bernsteinmuseum, Ribnitz

Andrea Wippermann, *Frösche*. Gold, 2001, 14 L X 8 W X 1 D.

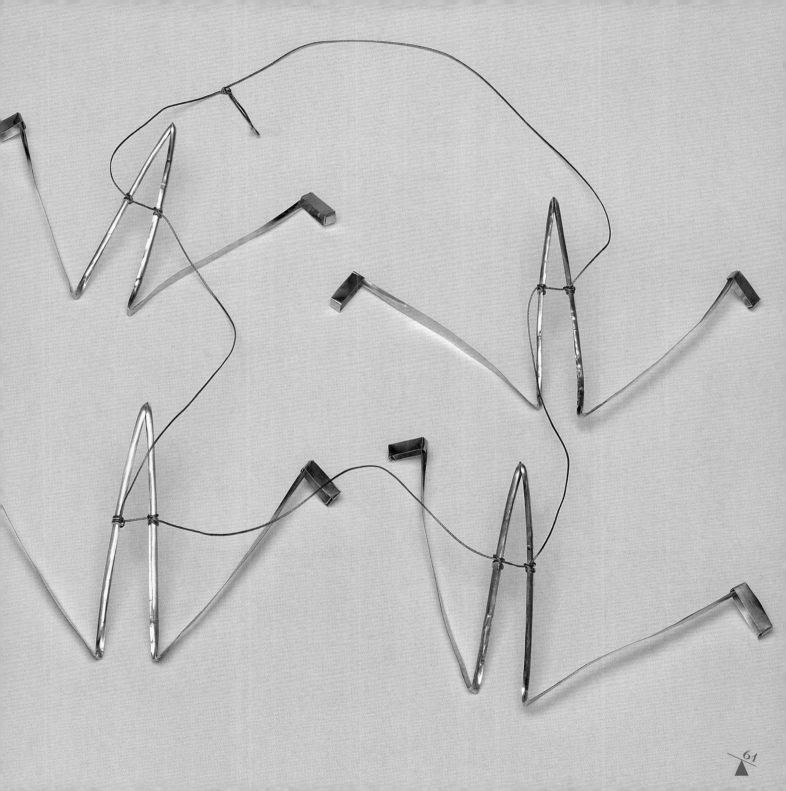

Exhibition Checklist

All dimensions listed in inches, height by width by depth. Dimensions may vary depending on if and how piece is worn.

Maru Almeida

Formation I: Layering
Hand-felted wool
2004
11 Diameter

Maru Almeida

Formation II: Crystals
Hand-felted wool
2004
7 Diameter

Maru Almeida

Formation III: Entangle
Hand-felted wool, peridot
2004
12 H X 7 W X 1 D

Jan Baum

Bird (Tattoo # 4)
Steel, silver
2004
Form only: 1⅜ H X 2 W

Jan Baum

Tattoo #1 (Maori #1)
Steel, silver
2004
Form only: 1¾ H X 2⅛ W

Jan Baum

Tattoo #2 (Maori #2)
Steel, silver
2004
Form only: 2H X 1¾ W

Iris Bodemer

No 04-001
Bronze, rose quartz, coral, citrine, pyrite, bone
2004
4½ H X 10 W X 2½ D

Iris Bodemer

No 04-002
Bronze, diamond crystal, onyx, garnet, wool
2004
10 H X 6 W X ⅓ D

Iris Bodemer

No 04-015
Gold, pearls, rubber, pebble
2004
8 H X 7 W X ½ D

Cynthia Cousens

Blue Tint
Acetate, monofilament
2004
33½ H X 35½ W X 1/3 D

Cynthia Cousens

Merge
Acetate, monofilament
2004
63 H X 13½ W X ¼ D

Cynthia Cousens

White on White (Study)
Paper, linen
2004
63 H X 13½ W X ¼ D

Bettina Dittlmann

Flowers
Iron, silver solder
2004
15 H X 12 W

Bettina Dittlmann

Four Leaf Clover
Iron, silver solder
2004
17 H X 14 W

Bettina Dittlmann

Hearts
Iron, silver solder
2004
19 H X 13 W

Helen Ellison-Dorion

Untitled #1
Sterling and fine silver, enamel, patina
2004
31 H X 12 W X 1½ D

Helen Ellison-Dorion

Untitled #2
Sterling and fine silver, enamel, patina
2004
72 H (extended) X 3 W X 2 D

Helen Ellison-Dorion

Untitled #3
Sterling and fine silver, enamel
2004
23 H X 11 W X 1 D

Sandra Enterline

Untitled
Oxidized silver, rubies, stainless steel
2004
Hanging length: 23

Sandra Enterline

Untitled
Silver, seed pearls
2004
Hanging length: 20

Sandra Enterline

Untitled
Silver
2004
11 Diameter

Nora Fok

Flower of Love
Nylon, black pearls
2004
27½ Diameter

Nora Fok

Hanging in Balance
Nylon, acrylic balls
2004
20 Diameter

Nora Fok

Looping Waves
Nylon
2004
13¾ Diameter

Maria Hanson

Family #1
Silver, gold leaf, cast resin
1994
Hanging length: 37½

Maria Hanson

Interlock #1
Oxidized silver, gold leaf, black ribbon
1994
Hanging length: 40⅓

Maria Hanson

Interlock #2
Silver, gold leaf, blue ribbon
1994
Hanging length: 35½

Dorothy Hogg

Neckpiece in the Artery Series
Silver, coral
2004
32 H X 12 W

Dorothy Hogg

Neckpiece in the Artery Series
Silver, felt
2004
40 H X 16 W

Dorothy Hogg

Tumbling Neckpiece
Silver, gold
2000
Hanging length: 27½

Svenja John

Bilabo
Polycarbonate, stainless steel
1999
Form only: 5¼ H X 3½ Diameter

Svenja John

Pimpollo
Polycarbonate, stainless steel
1999
Form only: 5 H X 2½ Diameter

Svenja John

Semila
Polycarbonate, stainless steel
2000
Form only: 4 H X ¹¹⁄₄ Diameter

Maria Phillips

Accumulate
Resin, silver plated copper, mixed media, stainless steel
2004
20 H X 9 W X 2 D

Maria Phillips

Flush
Steel, 18kt gold, gut, thread
2004
20 H X 10 W X 2 D

Maria Phillips

Parturient
Plaster, steel, gut, gold plated silver, silver
2004
22 H X 11 W X 1 D

Anika Smulovitz

White Collar # 1
Men's white shirt collar
2003
5 H X 6 W X 6 D

Anika Smulovitz

White Collar # 3
Men's white shirt collars
2003
2½ H X 5 W X 3½ D

Anika Smulovitz

White Collar #4
Men's white shirt collars
2003
13 H X 12 W X 12 D

Andrea Wippermann

Am Morgen
Gold
1996
15½ L X 3½ W X 1 D

Andrea Wippermann

Das Paar
Gold
1997
12 H X 14 W X 1 D

Andrea Wippermann

Frösche
Gold
2001
14 L X 8 W X 1 D